GREEN BOND MARKET SURVEY FOR CAMBODIA

INSIGHTS ON THE PERSPECTIVES OF INSTITUTIONAL INVESTORS AND UNDERWRITERS

SEPTEMBER 2022

ADB

ASIAN DEVELOPMENT BANK

CONTENTS

TABLE AND FIGURES

ACKNOWLEDGMENTS

The lead authors—Kosintr Puongsophol, Oth Marulou Gagni, and Alita Lestor—all from the Economic Research and Regional Cooperation Department (ERCD) of the Asian Development Bank, would like to particularly thank Satoru Yamadera, advisor, and Richard Supangan, senior economics officer, both of ERCD, for their support and contributions. Editing by Kevin Donahue. Design and layout by Prince Nicdao.

The lead authors would like to thank the ASEAN Secretariat and the Nomura Research Institute—its consultant under the ASEAN+3 Asian Bond Market Initiative's Technical Assistance Coordination Team, led by Jonathan Panggabean, Kengo Mizuno, Pimpadcha Kerdkokaew, and Dollaporn Khositphumiveth— for their inputs. Furthermore, the lead authors wish to acknowledge support from the Global Green Growth Institute team comprising Srinath Komarina, Hien Tran, Thinh Tran, Minh Tran, and Ha Nguyen.

Finally, we would like to express our heartfelt gratitude to Cambodian regulatory authorities and industry associations, as well as to all respondents, for their assistance with and participation in the survey. The local regulatory authorities include the Insurance Regulator of Cambodia, the National Bank of Cambodia, and the Securities and Exchange Regulator of Cambodia. Industry associations include the Association of Banks in Cambodia, among others.

ABBREVIATIONS

ABC	Association of Banks in Cambodia
ABMI	ASEAN+3 Asian Bond Markets Initiative
ADB	Asian Development Bank
ASEAN	Association of Southeast Asian Nations
ASEAN+3	ASEAN plus the People's Republic of China, Japan, and the Republic of Korea
CSFP	Cambodian Sustainable Finance Principles
NBC	National Bank of Cambodia
SERC	Securities and Exchange Regulator of Cambodia
USD	United States dollar

SUMMARY AND KEY FINDINGS

SURVEY HIGHLIGHTS

▶ The survey was conducted in January 2022 via an online platform and received a total of 32 responses from 2 brokerage firms, 9 financial advisors and underwriters, 18 insurance companies, as well as a single response each from the social security fund and the securities exchange. Multiple respondents from the same company responded to the survey.

▶ From the perspective of investors, renewable energy, energy efficiency, and water management are the sectors with the most growth potential, while underwriters also highlighted these sectors as well as waste management and the circular economy.

▶ The majority of investors favor smaller investment sizes of less than USD10 million, whereas underwriters favor issuance sizes of between USD11 million and USD50 million.

▶ Investors' primary motivations for investing in green bonds are the opportunities to diversify their investment portfolio and to improve their green image, whereas underwriters' clients are interested in lowering funding costs and boosting their green image.

▶ Investors and underwriters view the lack of resources, awareness, and clear regulatory guidance as significant obstacles to the development of the green bond market in Cambodia.

▶ As for policy options, investor and issuer respondents both emphasized the importance of government tax incentives, as well as preferential treatment for environmental, social, and governance financial products and an expansion of the green project pipeline.

▶ Development banks can play a variety of roles in catalyzing growth in the green bond market.

There is room for growth in the Cambodian green bond market. More than 60% of respondents, including underwriters and institutional investors, said they are interested in green bonds and are willing to explore investment and issuance opportunities. The main obstacles, however, are a lack of resources and capacities.

Renewable energy, energy efficiency, water management, and waste management and the circular economy are the sectors with the highest growth potential. Both institutional investors and underwriters agreed that renewable energy represents the sector with the highest growth potential. This was followed by energy efficiency, water management, and waste management and the circular economy (**Table**).

Table: Most Promising Sectors for Green Bonds in Cambodia
(share of respondents indicating agreement)
(%)

Investors			Underwriters		
Renewable Energy	Energy Efficiency	Water Management	Renewable Energy	Water Management	Waste Management and the Circular Economy
21	16	16	23	16	16

Source: Authors' compilation based on survey results.

Unlike underwriters, investors have a strong preference for smaller investment sizes. Almost 70% of investors are looking for an investment size of less than USD10 million per transaction, and 19% are seeking to invest up to USD50 million. On the other hand, almost 70% of underwriters are looking for issuance sizes of up to USD50 million.

Investors and clients of underwriters share similar motivations. All investors and underwriters who participated in the survey agreed that investing in and issuing green bonds can help an organization improve its green image. From an investors' point of view, investing in green bonds allows them to better diversify their portfolios, while issuers hope that issuing green bonds will result in lowered funding costs and an expanded investor base, albeit not immediately but rather potentially in the long run.

Critical impediments include a lack of resources, awareness, and regulatory guidance. Despite these motivations, both investors and underwriters stated that they lack the capacity and resources to invest in and advise their clients on these innovative financial products. Investors also stated that a lack of supply in the local market prevents them from investing in green bonds. Both categories of respondents agreed that local regulators should (i) publicly announce clear regulatory expectations that green bond market development is one of their top priorities and (ii) provide local market participants with the necessary support.

A clear investment mandate and the expansion of eligible issuers are also important. Almost all survey respondents agreed that tax incentives and subsidies for green bond investors and issuers are critical to increasing green bond issuance and investment. Investors would benefit greatly from a subsidy for issuers to engage an external reviewer to label their green bonds, as this would provide them with additional assurance that they are investing in a credible green bond. Meanwhile, both underwriters and investors agreed that expanding the pipeline of green projects and attracting new issuers, particularly corporate issuers, to green bond markets is critical. Underwriters also believed that increased investor demand was critical to encouraging more green bond issuance. Preferential buying by public pension funds and central banks would, in fact, demonstrate leading by example.

Development partners can play an important role in promoting green finance. All respondents agreed that development partners such as the Asian Development Bank (ADB) and Global Green Growth Institute can play a variety of roles in assisting Cambodia's green finance market's development. Along with serving as a knowledge partner, multilateral institutions can provide technical assistance to assist local companies in issuing green bonds and identifying eligible green projects and expenditures. Additionally, ADB can invest in green bonds and/or make green loans to domestic entities.

INTRODUCTION

Background and Objective

The Asian Development Bank (ADB) is collaborating closely with the Association of Southeast Asian Nations (ASEAN), the People's Republic of China, Japan, and the Republic of Korea—collectively known as ASEAN+3—to promote the development of local currency bond markets and regional bond market integration through the Asian Bond Markets Initiative (ABMI). The ABMI was established in 2002 to bolster the resilience of ASEAN+3 financial systems by developing local currency bond markets as an alternative source to foreign-currency-denominated, short-term bank loans for long-term investment financing.

ADB, as Secretariat for the ABMI, is implementing a regional technical assistance program to promote sustainable local currency bond market development with support from the People's Republic of China's Poverty Reduction and Regional Cooperation Fund. This technical assistance was developed and is being implemented with guidance from ASEAN+3 finance ministers and central bank governors, and in accordance with the ABMI Medium-Term Road Map for 2019–2022.

This survey report, conducted in collaboration with the Global Green Growth Institute, aims to assess institutional investors' interest in green bonds issued in Cambodia, as well as the perspectives of local arrangers and underwriters on their clients' interest in green bond issuance. The survey aims to identify market drivers, impediments, and development priorities for Cambodia's sustainable finance market to assist development partners in identifying potential areas of support to accelerate the development of Cambodia's sustainable finance market.

Methodologies

In January 2022, ADB and the Global Green Growth Institute conducted the survey via an online platform and received a total of 32 responses from 2 brokerage firms (proprietary trading), 9 financial advisors and underwriters, 18 insurance companies, and a single response each from the social security fund and the securities exchange. Multiple respondents from the same company responded to the survey.

OVERVIEW OF CAMBODIA'S SUSTAINABLE BOND MARKET

Bond Market

The bond market of Cambodia is in the nascent stage of development. Cambodia's first domestic corporate bond was issued in 2018 by Hattha Kaksekar Limited, a microfinance company, at an initial amount of KHR120 billion.[1] This paved the way for subsequent bond issuances in the country. The government's tax incentive program for first-time securities listings will be available until 2025 as a way to expedite the capital market's development. As of June 2022, there were seven corporate bonds from five issuers listed on the Cambodia Securities Exchange, with an aggregate issuance volume of KHR452 billion.

Among the six issues, one issuance by Telcotech Ltd., a digital communication company, was offered at the amount of KHR80 billion in August 2021 and has been listed on the Cambodia Securities Exchange since September 2021.[2] This is the first corporate bond offered to qualified investors in Cambodia.

The government also plans to resume issuance of government securities in 2022—the most recent Treasury bill issuance took place in 2006. Meanwhile, there have been no sustainable bonds issued in Cambodia yet.

Laws and Regulations

Corporate bond regulation is provided by the (i) Law on Issuance and Trading of Non-Government Securities, (ii) Prakas on Public Offering of Debt Securities, and (iii) Prakas on Debt Securities Offering for Qualified Investors. Even though none of these laws or *prakas* (regulations) incorporate sustainable bond matters, the Securities and Exchange Regulator of Cambodia (SERC) has announced publicly that sustainable debt securities can be issued under existing regulations. SERC will soon issue complementary guidelines on the issuance of green, social, and sustainable bonds to inform potential issuers on the regulations and standards they may apply for their thematic bond issuance.

The SERC launched the *Green Bond Issuance Handbook*, with support from ADB, in July 2022. The handbook introduces alternative green definitions and certifications, including the standards and taxonomies of ASEAN and other international bodies, such as the International Capital Market Association and the Climate Bonds Initiative, and provides potential issuers with details on the green bond issuance process, including selecting a green definition, preparing the bond framework, managing the use of proceeds, making disclosure, and engaging an external reviewer.

---

[1] Hattha Kaksekar Limited. "The First Cambodian Corporate Bond No. 1" to be issued to the public by Hattha Kaksekar Limited. Press release.

[2] Credit Guarantee & Investment Facility. 2021. CGIF guarantees first KHR bond offered through private placement for Telcotech Ltd., a landmark transaction in Cambodia. 25 August. Press release.

RECENT INITIATIVES ON SUSTAINABLE FINANCE

The sustainable finance market in Cambodia was launched in 2016 when the Association of Banks in Cambodia (ABC) commenced an initiative to develop and strengthen financial sector safeguards and risk management standards in response to potential social and environmental impacts emanating from the private sector. The decision was made to take a bottom-up approach that would be led and owned by banks with assistance from international partners. The Cambodian Sustainable Finance Initiative was launched on 19 September 2016.[3] The Cambodia Sustainable Finance Principles (CSFP) were subsequently approved by the ABC and distributed to all member banks in October 2018. By December of the same year, the majority of Cambodian banks had adopted the CSFP after the ABC issued guidance urging all member banks to do so. The ABC also released the revised version of the CSFP Implementation Guidelines in February 2019 to serve as a basis for Cambodian banks and microfinance institutions in developing their own sustainable finance approaches in line with the CSFP.

The nine CSFP aim to protect the environment, people, and cultural heritage of Cambodia:

(i) **Principle 1.** We will assess and manage environmental risks relating to climate change, pollution, and waste management, as well as protect our critical natural resources.

(ii) **Principle 2.** We will assess and manage risks that could potentially negatively impact our people, in particular local communities, workers, and indigenous and minority populations.

(iii) **Principle 3.** We will assess and manage risks that could potentially negatively impact aspects of our cultural heritage, including our language, culture, traditions, and monuments.

(iv) **Principle 4.** We will increase the financial awareness and literacy of the Cambodian people and improve our approach to customer and client protection.

(v) **Principle 5.** We will expand our reach to those who previously had either no or limited access to the formal banking sector, and provide more innovative solutions to improve banking access and service levels.

(vi) **Principle 6.** We will finance innovations that create efficiencies to improve existing traditional sectors and business activities and develop new green economy activities.

(vii) **Principle 7.** We will seek to build capacities across banks to deliver on our commitments to our customers and communities and raise awareness about sustainable, inclusive finance.

---

3   The Association of Banks in Cambodia. The Cambodian Sustainable Finance Initiative.

(viii) **Principle 8.** We will manage our own environmental and social footprints and request similar standards from our suppliers.

(ix) **Principle 9.** We will annually report individual and sectoral progress against these commitments to hold ourselves accountable and share the story and outcomes of our journey and the value we believe can be created for Cambodia.

Meanwhile, the National Bank of Cambodia (NBC) demonstrated its commitment to promoting green finance in early 2020 by becoming a member of the Network of Central Banks and Supervisors for Greening the Financial System. The network's purpose is to help strengthen global efforts to meet the goals of the Paris Agreement and enhance the capacities of financial systems to manage risks and mobilize capital for green and low-carbon investments in the broader context of environmentally sustainable development.[4]

In February 2022, the NBC announced its support for the launch of the Bank for International Settlements-managed Asian Green Bond Fund. The fund's objective is to purchase high-quality green bonds issued by sovereign states, international financial institutions, and corporations. As a member of the advisory committee, the NBC will be among the fund's first subscribers, marking an innovative step toward sustainable financing.[5]

In terms of capital market development, the SERC, in collaboration with ADB, published the *Green Bond Issuance Handbook* in July 2022 to provide clarity and guidance on green bond issuance processes. The SERC has also embarked on several initiatives to promote sustainable capital market development in Cambodia, including organizing a series of webinars and workshops in partnership with development partners and stakeholders.

On 26 May 2022, the SERC announced that sustainable debt securities can be issued under existing regulations.[6]

[4]   Network of Central Banks and Supervisors for Greening the Financial System. Origin and Purpose.

[5]   May Kunmakara. 2022. NBC Heralds Eco-Friendly Investment Fund. *Phnom Penh Post*. 27 February.

[6]   May Kunmakara. 2022. Issue Green Bonds, Build Green Ecosystem. *Phnom Penh Post*. 26 May.

SURVEY RESULTS

The survey was conducted in January 2022 among local institutional investors (e.g., fund managers, financial institutions, and insurance companies) and local underwriters and advisors. A summary of the survey's findings is given below.

Institutional Investors

The survey began by asking about respondent firms' interest in investing in green bonds. The majority of respondents indicated there was interest in green bonds even with limited awareness and resources at present, while almost 25% of respondents were not interested at this stage due to a lack of awareness, capital limitations, an insufficient supply of green bonds in the market, inherent risks, a lack of relevance to business operations, or green bonds not yet being a part of the company's plans (**Figure 1**). Interestingly, one insurance company indicated that despite being in the exploration stage, albeit with limited awareness and resources, it is the company's objective to achieve net-zero carbon emissions.

When asked about ticket size, 69% of respondents indicated a preference for investments of less than USD10 million, while 19% indicated a willingness to invest up to USD50 million per transaction (**Figure 2**). Only 6% of respondents indicated uncertainty regarding the amount, depending on the credit

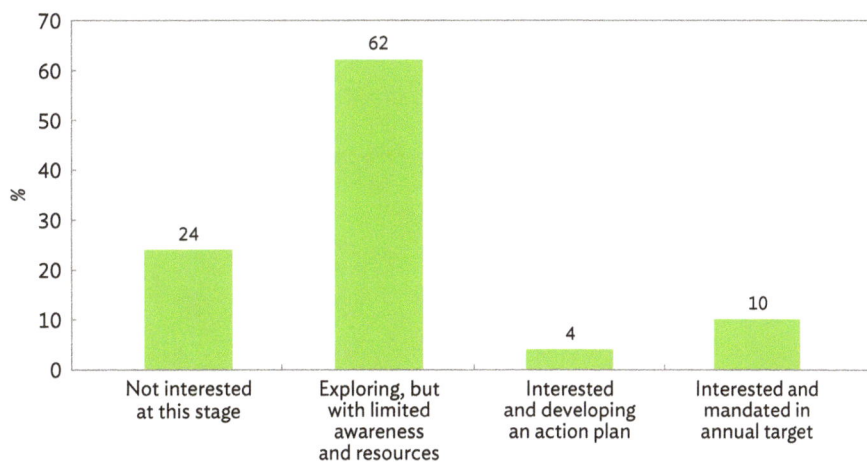

Figure 1: Interest in Investing in Green Bonds

Source: Authors' compilation based on survey results.

Figure 2: Optimal Investment Size

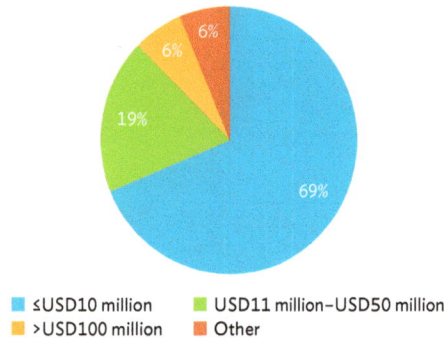

- ■ ≤USD10 million
- ■ USD11 million–USD50 million
- ■ >USD100 million
- ■ Other

Source: Authors' compilation based on survey results.

Sustainable Development Goals into their investment strategy (**Figure 3**).

Investors were asked to identify any significant barriers they believed might prevent them from investing in green bonds in order to assist ADB and Cambodian regulators in facilitating the development of the green bond market (**Figure 4**). The biggest obstacles cited were a lack of policy direction from regulators, an internal lack of resources and guidance on these types of investment, and the dearth of green bonds available in the domestic market. The lack of obvious advantages of green bonds over conventional bonds was also considered to be a significant barrier to investment.

quality of the issuer and the bond terms, while another 6% indicated a preference of over USD100 million. These findings are consistent with green bond market surveys conducted in most other ASEAN countries.

When asked why investors are interested in exploring possible investment opportunities in green bonds, the majority of investors cited diversification of their investment portfolio as the most crucial consideration, followed by an improvement in their organization's green reputation and the chance to incorporate the

Investors consider the historical performance of an issuer as the primary factor when making an investment decision (**Figure 5**). The next most critical considerations for green bond investors are valuation and pricing, company profile or management team, and credit rating. The majority of investors also believe that brand association and the reinforcement of positive attributes about the brand are crucial in making investment decisions.

Figure 3: Key Motivations for Investing in Green Bonds

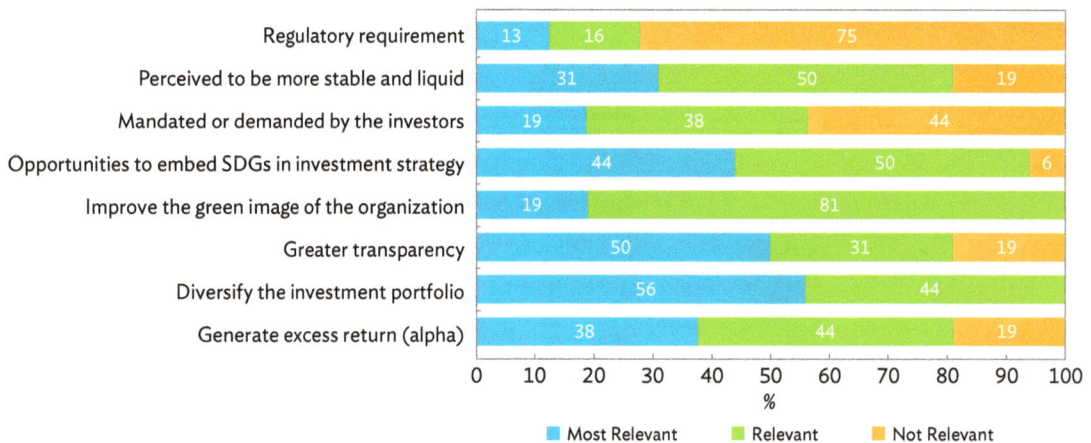

SDG = Sustainable Development Goal.
Source: Authors' compilation based on survey results.

Figure 4: Main Obstacles to Investing in Green Bonds

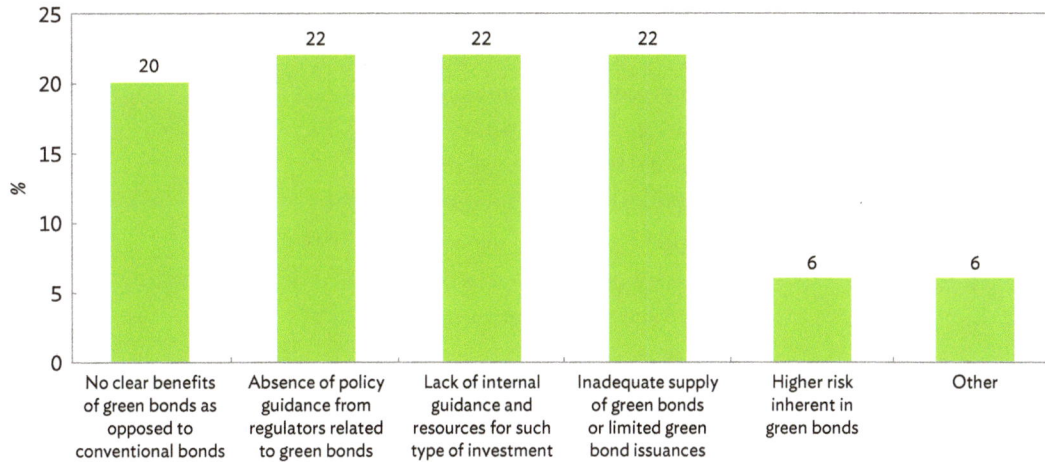

Source: Authors' compilation based on survey results.

Figure 5: Key Considerations for Investing in Green Bonds

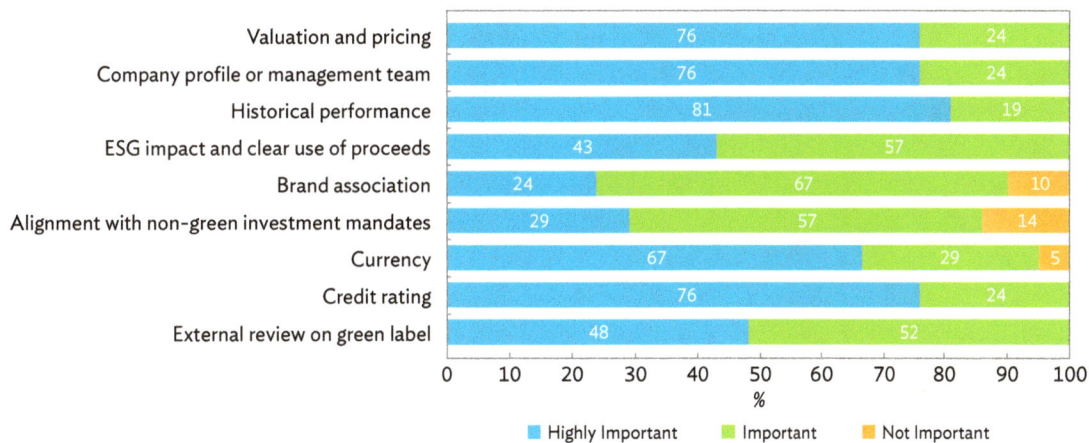

ESG = environmental, social, and governance.
Source: Authors' compilation based on survey results.

Respondents were requested to select up to three options that they felt could encourage the growth of Cambodia's green bond market. Nearly 90% of respondents recommended that the government implement tax incentives and/or subsidies to entice investors to hold more green bonds (**Figure 6**). Under the 2022 Anukret (Sub-Decree) on Tax Incentives in the Securities Sector, the government will offer additional special tax incentives to businesses that issue securities (both equities and bonds) to finance green and sustainable development projects in priority sectors, as determined by the Ministry of Economy and Finance.

Meanwhile, almost 50% of respondents indicated that an external review of green bonds framework, as well as regulatory support and

Figure 6: Policy Mechanisms That Would Increase Green Bond Investments

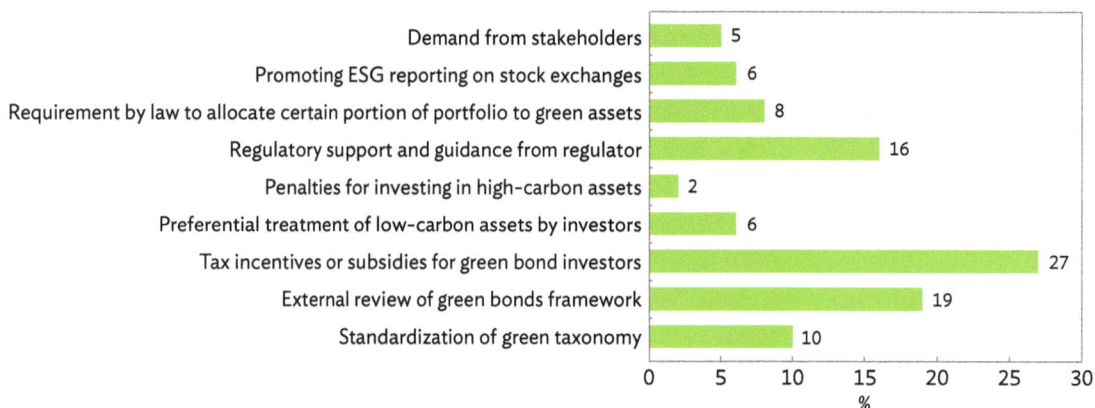

Policy Mechanism	%
Demand from stakeholders	5
Promoting ESG reporting on stock exchanges	6
Requirement by law to allocate certain portion of portfolio to green assets	8
Regulatory support and guidance from regulator	16
Penalties for investing in high-carbon assets	2
Preferential treatment of low-carbon assets by investors	6
Tax incentives or subsidies for green bond investors	27
External review of green bonds framework	19
Standardization of green taxonomy	10

ESG = environmental, social, and governance.
Source: Authors' compilation based on survey results.

guidance, would significantly assist investors in making green investment decisions.

The survey further investigated which types of green bond issuers respondents are interested in. Local institutional investors indicated that they are most interested in corporate issuers such as financial institutions, followed by development banks and the government (**Figure 7**). For nonfinancial institutions, respondents

believe that renewable energy (21%), energy efficiency (16%), and water management (16%) offer the greatest investment potential in Cambodia (**Figure 8**).

A majority of respondents emphasized the critical importance of government and regulatory policy clarity to increase private financing, with over 70% of respondents believing this to be the most important factor.

Figure 7: Level of Local Investor Interest by Issuer Type

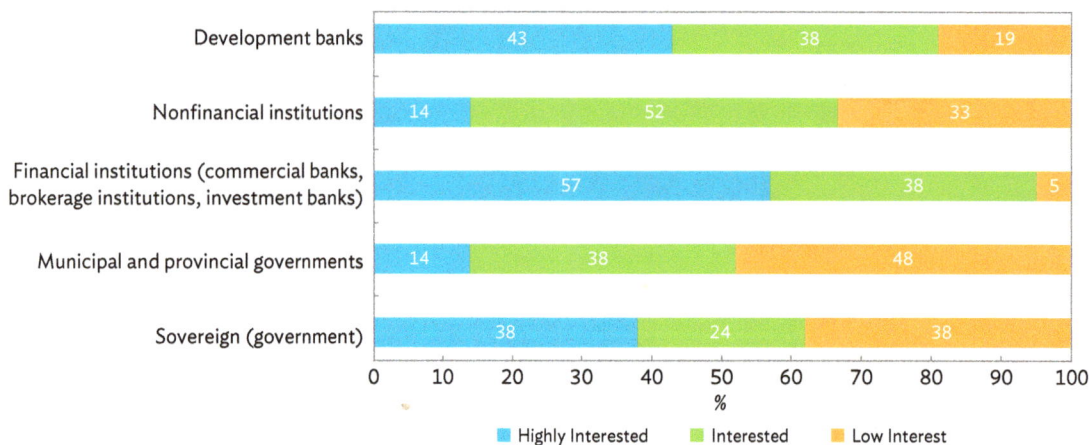

Issuer Type	Highly Interested	Interested	Low Interest
Development banks	43	38	19
Nonfinancial institutions	14	52	33
Financial institutions (commercial banks, brokerage institutions, investment banks)	57	38	5
Municipal and provincial governments	14	38	48
Sovereign (government)	38	24	38

Source: Authors' compilation based on survey results.

Figure 8: Sectors with Most Potential for Green Bond Investments

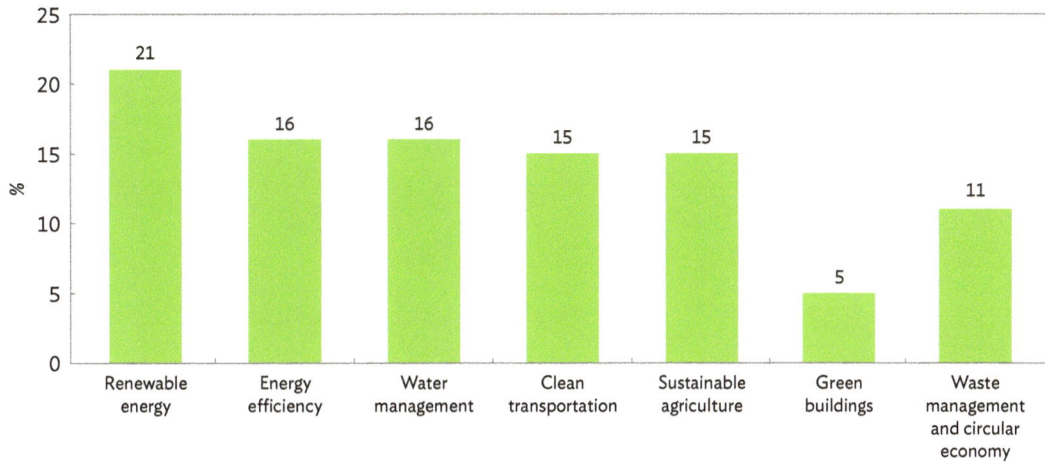

Source: Authors' compilation based on survey results.

The majority of respondents identified tax incentives for green bond investors and an expanded pipeline of eligible projects as the most crucial policy options in supporting the development of the green bond market in Cambodia (**Figure 9**). Additionally, these will encourage investors and make green bonds an attractive investment.

Regarding capacity development, respondents nearly unanimously agreed that investors and asset managers require additional training (**Figure 10**). It is also widely held that deal teams inside investment banks and securities firms should be trained to gain a better understanding of green bonds. This would lead to an increase in the supply of green bonds to meet investor demand.

Figure 9: Policy Options for Green Bond Market Development

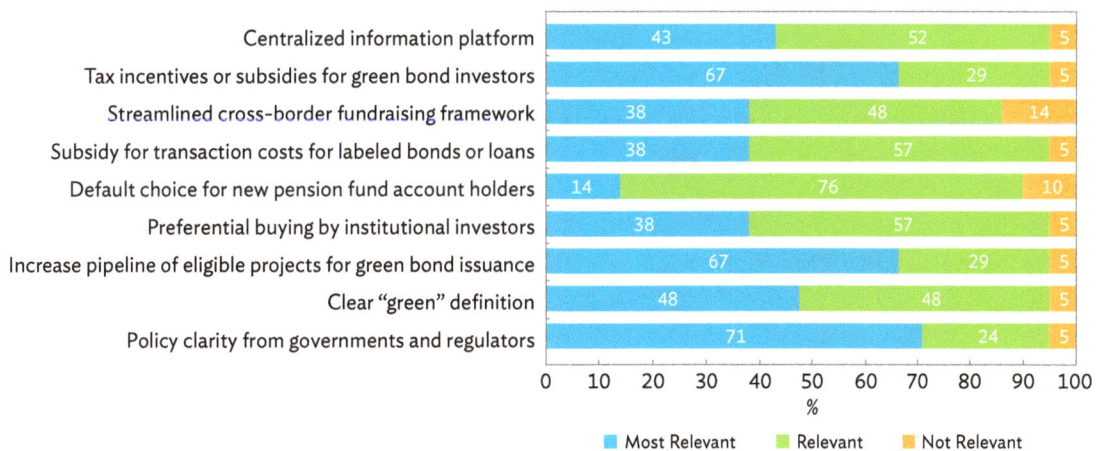

Source: Authors' compilation based on survey results.

Figure 10: Capacity Building—Who Should Be Trained?

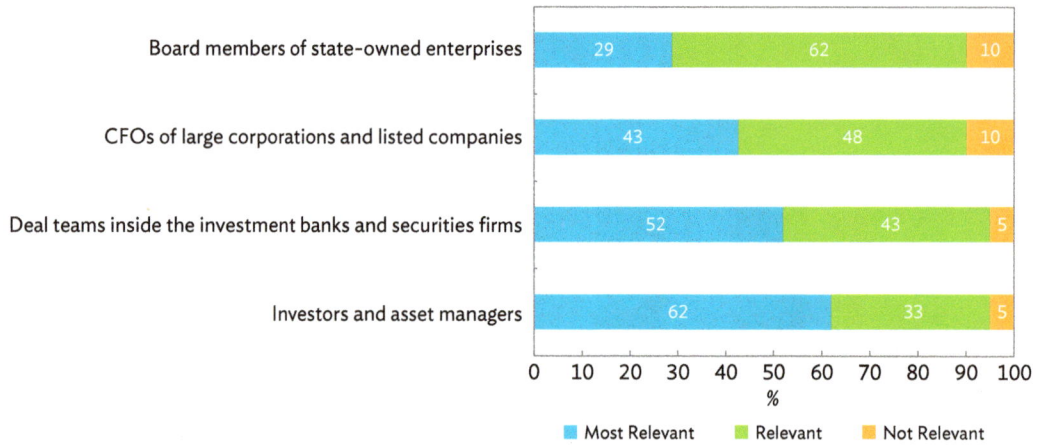

CFO = chief financial officer.
Source: Authors' compilation based on survey results.

The majority of Cambodian investors intend to invest in the wider ASEAN region (**Figure 11**). Singapore, Indonesia, Thailand, and Viet Nam are the preferred investment destinations for those interested. When asked about preferences for a bond's underlying currency, over 58% of respondents chose the United States dollar, followed by the Singaporean dollar at 16% (**Figure 12**).

Figure 11: Investor Interest in Regional Investment

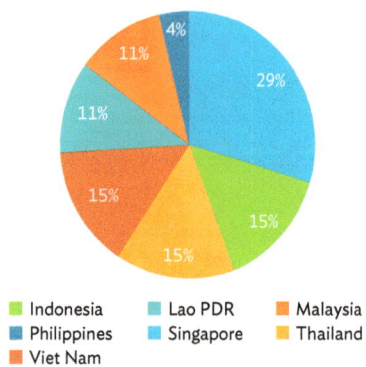

Lao PDR = Lao People's Democratic Republic.
Source: Authors' compilation based on survey results.

Figure 12: Preferred Underlying Currencies

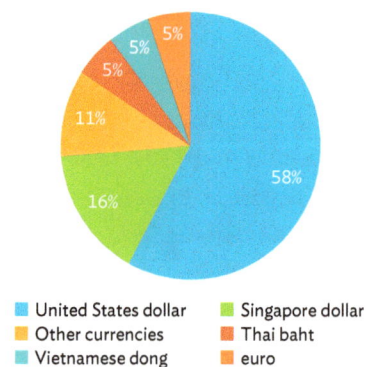

Source: Authors' compilation based on survey results.

Advisors and Underwriters

This section examines the interest of potential green bond issuers, the most promising economic sectors, and the various types of potential issuers based on responses from local advisors and underwriters.

On the supply side, a two-thirds majority of respondents' clients are exploring possible green bond issuances, but with limited awareness and resources, while 16% of respondents indicated that their clients want to issue green bond within a year. This may be an area where development partners such as ADB can assist interested entities with technical assistance and capacity building (**Figure 13**).

In terms of issuance size, almost 70% of respondents indicated an optimal issuance size for green bonds of between USD11 million and USD50 million, while 25% of respondents shared that the optimal deal size should be below USD10 million (**Figure 14**). In contrast, nearly 70% of responses from local institutional investors indicated that they seek investments of less than USD10 million per transaction.

Figure 14: Optimal Issuance Size

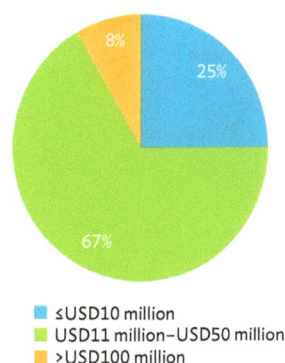

- ≤USD10 million
- USD11 million–USD50 million
- >USD100 million

Source: Authors' compilation based on survey results.

All of the respondents mentioned that their clients prefer issuance of green bonds in hard currencies. Half of the respondents confirmed that their clients are interested in issuing green bonds in other countries, particularly Japan, Thailand, Singapore, Malaysia, and Indonesia.

Renewable energy represents the sector with the greatest opportunity for green bond issuance in Cambodia over the next 3 years, according to survey respondents (**Figure 15**). In addition, 16% of all respondents agreed that water

Figure 13: Interest in Issuing Green Bonds

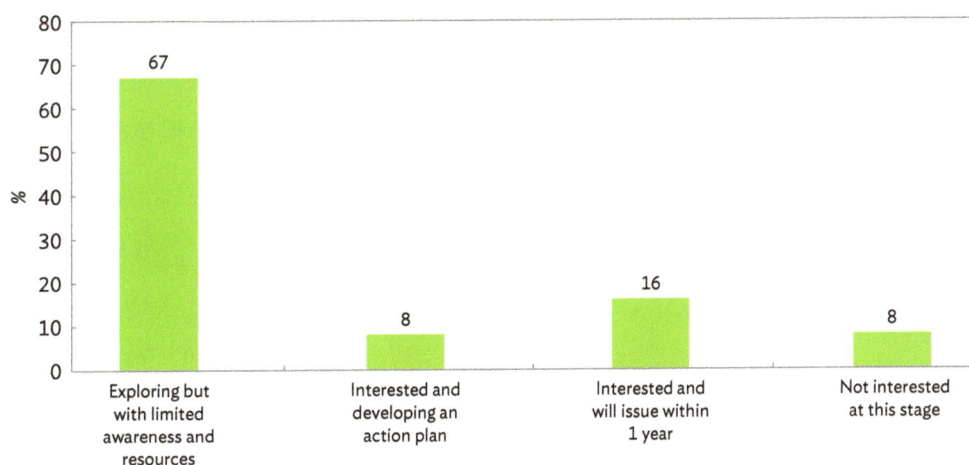

Source: Authors' compilation based on survey results.

Figure 15: Most Promising Sectors for Green Bonds Issuance

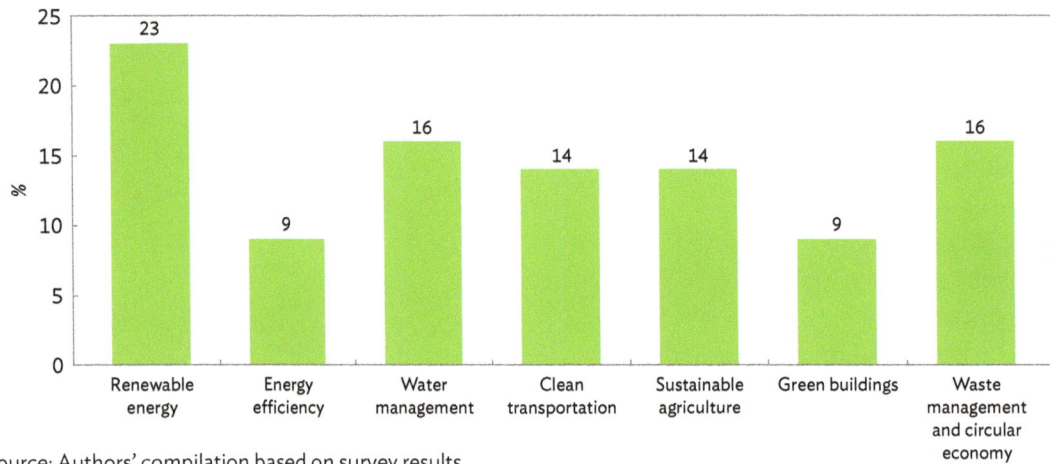

Renewable energy: 23, Energy efficiency: 9, Water management: 16, Clean transportation: 14, Sustainable agriculture: 14, Green buildings: 9, Waste management and circular economy: 16 (%)

Source: Authors' compilation based on survey results.

management and waste management and the circular economy hold significant development potential for the Cambodian green bond market. These findings are consistent with the perspective of institutional investors regarding the sectors with the greatest potential for green bond investment in Cambodia.

When asked about motivations for green bond issuance, the majority of respondents cited

the opportunity to attract new investors and reduce funding costs as the two most important factors. Meanwhile, all respondents agreed that, to a lesser extent, green bond issuance could result in an issuer's improved green image (**Figure 16**).

Concerning market development, the majority of respondents identified a lack of awareness as a clear impediment to their clients issuing

Figure 16: Key Motivations for Issuing Green Bonds

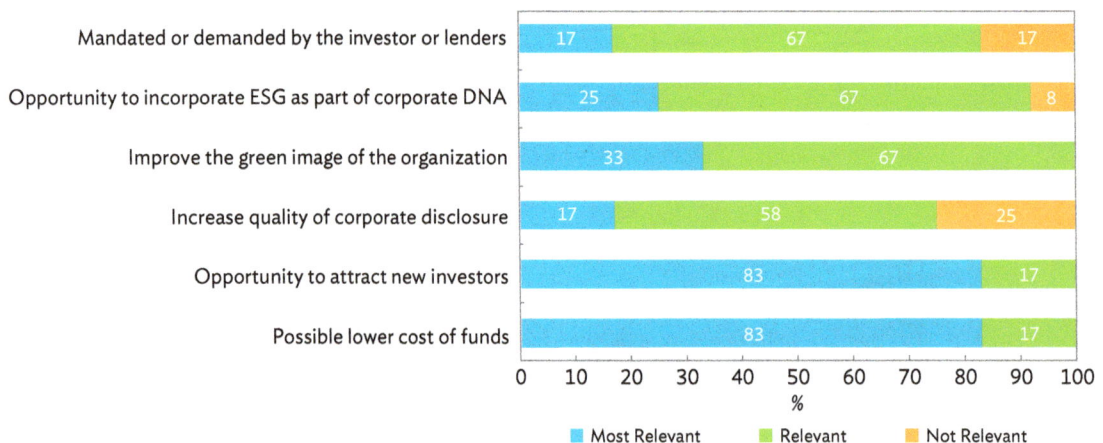

Motivation	Most Relevant	Relevant	Not Relevant
Mandated or demanded by the investor or lenders	17	67	17
Opportunity to incorporate ESG as part of corporate DNA	25	67	8
Improve the green image of the organization	33	67	
Increase quality of corporate disclosure	17	58	25
Opportunity to attract new investors	83	17	
Possible lower cost of funds	83	17	

ESG = environmental, social, and governance.
Source: Authors' compilation based on survey results.

green bonds (**Figure 17**). Another significant impediment was the absence of policy guidance from regulators in relation to green bonds and a lack of internal resources to consider new products. Interestingly, one respondent mentioned that there was a shallow investor base.

Respondents were then asked to identify the primary policy mechanisms that could facilitate increased green bond issuance in Cambodia. The majority of respondents indicated tax incentives or subsidies for green bond issuers as the primary factor, followed by standardization of a green taxonomy (**Figure 18**). Other important

Figure 17: Main Obstacles to the Issuance of Green Bonds

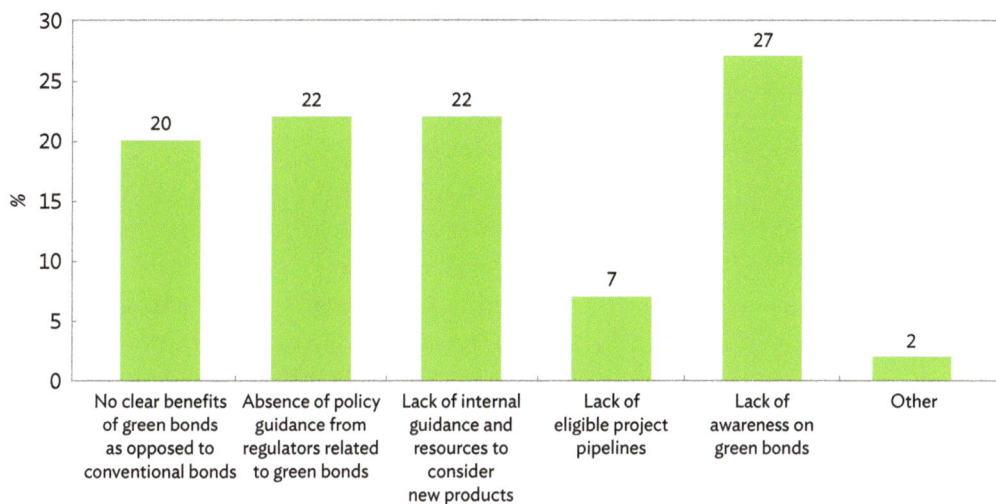

Source: Authors' compilation based on survey results.

Figure 18: Key Policy Drivers for Increased Green Bond Issuance

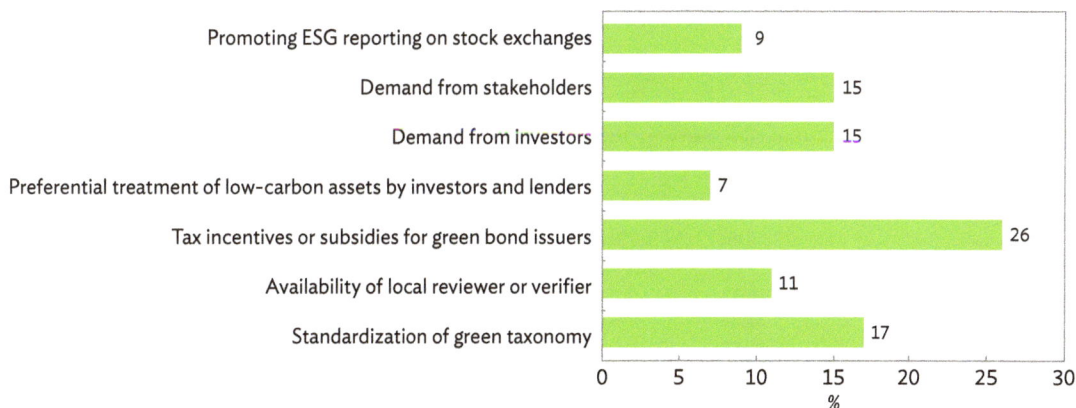

ESG = environmental, social, and governance.
Source: Authors' compilation based on survey results.

factors include demand from stakeholders and investors, as well as the availability of a local reviewer or verifier.

When asked about potential investors, 75% of respondents believed that development partners such as ADB could significantly contribute to the development of the local green bond market by investing in green bonds issued by their clients (**Figure 19**). Meanwhile, half of the respondents agreed that insurance companies, particularly those that are subsidiaries of international insurers, should invest in green bonds, with nearly 50% believing that insurance companies could play a significant role in facilitating the issuance of longer-term debt. Additionally, respondents believed that if retail investors gained a better understanding of environmental, social, and governance investing, they would be able to invest in green bonds via pension and social security funds, and that these funds could become mainstream investors.

Similar to institutional investors, underwriters and advisors believe that tax incentives for issuers and investors—as well as a subsidy for transaction costs for labeled bonds and loans

and preferential purchasing by institutional investors—are required for Cambodia's green bond market to develop (**Figure 20**). In addition, respondents believe that an increased pipeline of eligible projects could be a significant factor in the issuance of green bonds. It is essential that local advisors and underwriters have a thorough understanding of the green bond issuance process and the eligibility criteria for green projects so that they can advise clients and assist them in identifying assets, projects, and expenditures that comply with international principles and standards.

In terms of capacity building, all respondents believe that board members of state-owned enterprises would benefit from training to better understand green bonds and the importance of including them in their financing strategy (**Figure 21**). Training is also needed for the chief financial officers of large corporations and listed companies, deal teams inside investment banks and securities firms, and investor and asset managers. Meanwhile, all respondents also believed that investors and asset managers should be trained to increase demand for green bonds.

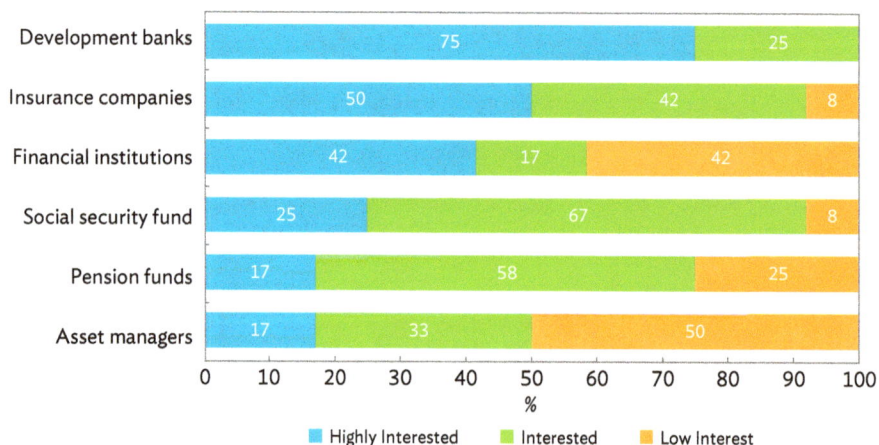

Figure 19: Preferred Investors in Green Bonds

Source: Authors' compilation based on survey results.

Figure 20: Policy Options for Green Bond Market Development

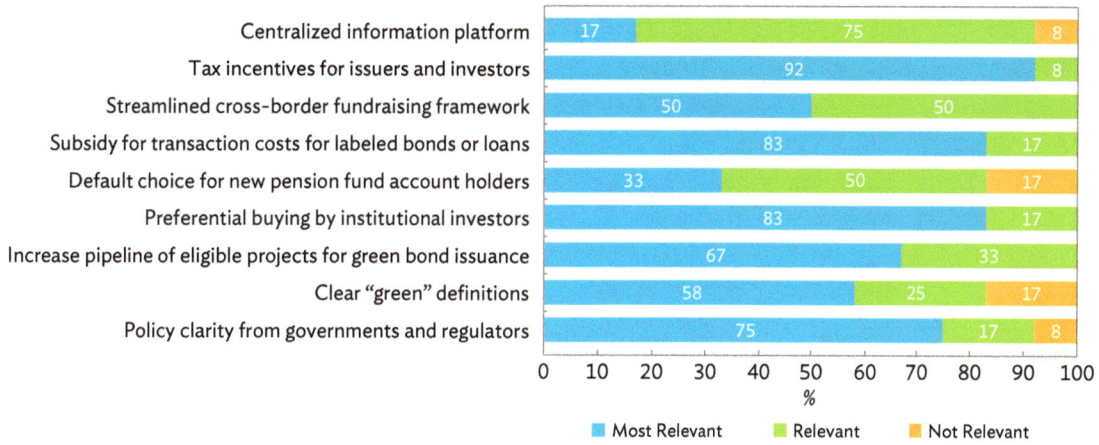

Policy Option	Most Relevant	Relevant	Not Relevant
Centralized information platform	17	75	8
Tax incentives for issuers and investors	92		8
Streamlined cross-border fundraising framework	50	50	
Subsidy for transaction costs for labeled bonds or loans	83	17	
Default choice for new pension fund account holders	33	50	17
Preferential buying by institutional investors	83	17	
Increase pipeline of eligible projects for green bond issuance	67	33	
Clear "green" definitions	58	25	17
Policy clarity from governments and regulators	75	17	8

Legend: ■ Most Relevant ■ Relevant ■ Not Relevant

Source: Authors' compilation based on survey results.

Figure 21: Capacity Building—Who Should Be Trained?

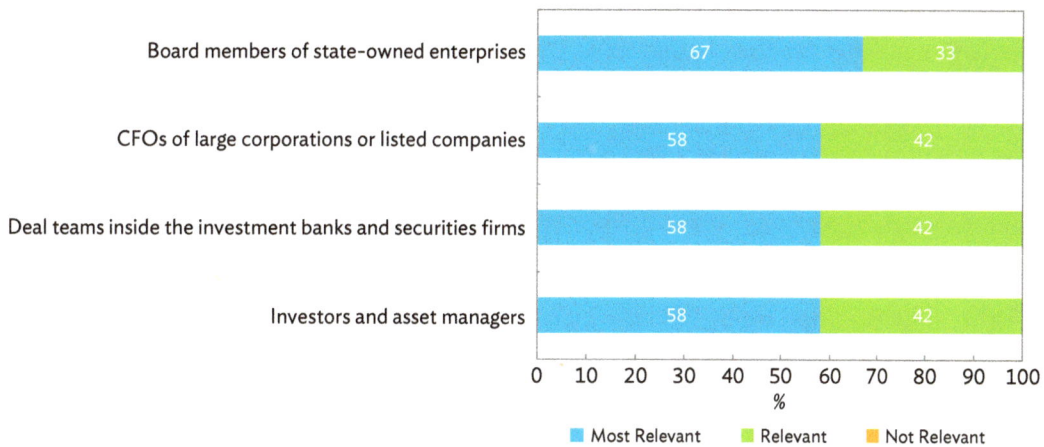

	Most Relevant	Relevant	Not Relevant
Board members of state-owned enterprises	67	33	
CFOs of large corporations or listed companies	58	42	
Deal teams inside the investment banks and securities firms	58	42	
Investors and asset managers	58	42	

Legend: ■ Most Relevant ■ Relevant ■ Not Relevant

CFO = chief financial officer.
Source: Authors' compilation based on survey results.

WHAT ADB CAN DO TO HELP

Respondents identified several ways in which ADB could assist the Cambodian green bond market's development. These beneficial recommendations can be classified as follows.

As a Knowledge Partner

ADB could provide technical assistance such as green bond framework development, external reviews, capacity development, systems development to monitor the use of bond proceeds, preparation of post-issuance reports, and the sharing of best practices that have been successfully adopted within and outside the region.

ADB could work with regulators and potential investors to establish proper guidelines for the green bond market. Furthermore, ADB could effectively partner with the Government of Cambodia to develop or establish a clear framework; promote green investment benefits; and advise on the creation of laws and rules for these types of investments, including the setting of investment thresholds.

As an Investor

ADB can encourage relevant regulators to require or incentivize private institutions like commercial banks, insurance companies, and fund management companies to invest in green bonds. ADB can help increase the visibility of bankable projects in Cambodia and provide credit guarantee to investors.

Respondents also suggested that ADB could support equity investments to promote social and economic development, create various investment opportunities, and provide regulatory support.

FINAL WORD FROM SURVEY RESPONDENTS

Survey respondents were asked to give some final words on green bond market development in Cambodia. The following list comprises a few highlighted responses:

▶ Our company will strongly support the green bond project.

▶ We are excited for the future to come.

▶ Green bond issuances enable establishment of sustainable investment fund.

▶ Green represents life and sustainability.

▶ Green buildings shall be promoted given that these commercial buildings are well developed. Clean transportation may be another priority [as transportation] releases pollution into the environment. But a country like Cambodia has not yet done many things to encourage these sectors.

▶ [It is necessary to] reduce the complexity of process guidelines and reporting.

▶ Strong support from the related parties is needed to reduce issuance cost and simplify the issuance process (e.g., reduce some unnecessary paperwork in order to speed up the process).

▶ Interest rates required by potential issuers tend to be lower than those required by investors.

▶ The development of a green bond market across the region is not going as fast as it should. It requires collaboration from important stakeholders such as the government, private sector, and development partners across the region to come together and [accelerate the process].

▶ Green bonds can support our country's economy in the future.

▶ We should consider the matching of the interest rate, currency, and tenor. The label of the bond [should] also align with the Paris Agreement.

▶ Cambodia needs more energy supply given its high electricity prices. However, corporate governance issues need to be resolved.

▶ The more thought we put into a green environment, the more sustainable living we will have.

NEXT STEPS

This survey revealed that the majority of respondents, among both investors and underwriters, are committed to becoming more environmentally friendly. Additional efforts, however, are required, particularly in terms of capacity building for relevant stakeholders, the expansion of an eligible project pipeline and issuer base, greater incentives (including tax incentive for both local investors and issuers), and technical assistance from development partners. As highlighted in this report, a majority of investors and underwriters are interested in green bonds but lack the capacity and resources to bring this innovative financial product to the market. Development partners can play a crucial role in providing technical assistance to Cambodian stakeholders.

As Secretariat of the ABMI, ADB will continue to work closely with local regulatory bodies to establish and strengthen the ecosystem necessary for the development of Cambodia's sustainable finance market, including capacity building, the publication of handbooks, and technical assistance to aid issuers on their sustainable finance journey.

www.ingramcontent.com/pod-product-compliance
Lightning Source LLC
Chambersburg PA
CBHW050058220326
41599CB00045B/7460